登 长 城 纪 念

A COMVEMORATIVE CERTIFICATE FOR ASCENDING THE GREAT WALL IN CHINA

不到長城非好漢

NOT A PLUCKY HERO UNTIL ONE REACHES THE GREAT WALL

我登上了長城

I HAVE ASCENDED THE GREAT WALL

颁 发 给
This is to certify that ....

攀 登 长 城 日 期
did climb the Great Wall on ....

中国之魂
Soul of China

万里长城留念
Memory of The Ten -Thousand-Li Great Wall

前　　言

　　在中華大地上，舉世聞名的萬里長城，象一條奔騰的巨龍，騰起于鴨綠江畔，向西越過巍巍的群山，茫茫的草原，跨過浩瀚的大漠，奔向白雪皚皚的天山之麓。以它异常艱巨的工程和磅礴的氣勢把北國風光點綴得更加絢麗多彩。

　　長城是中國古代偉大的軍事防御工程，用以抵御北方的游牧民族。從公元前七世紀的春秋戰國直至公元十七世紀的明代末年，沿續了兩千年之久。先后有二十幾個王朝修築過長城，其中工程最大的為秦始皇統一中國后修築的秦長城，漢武帝修築的漢長城，明太祖修築的明長城。至明代，長城那些著名的雄關要塞已構成了完整的軍事防御體系，建有衛所城、鎮城、路城、營城、邊關、敵臺、戰臺、烽火臺、水門等等。東起鴨綠江口，西至甘肅嘉峪關，總長度約為一萬二千七百多華里。長城大都建于山嶺之顛，沿着山脊把蜿蜒無盡的山勢勾畫出優美的曲綫輪廓，城上無盡的敵臺，和矗立于嶺上的烽火臺遙相呼應，萬里長城以它磅礴的氣勢奔騰于崇山峻嶺之中，成百座雄關、隘口，成千上萬的雄壯敵臺、烽火臺連成一體，其巍峨壯觀的磅礴氣勢令人們嘆為觀止，感嘆中華民族的勤勞、智慧、和杰出偉大。

　　長城在中國歷史上奔騰飛越了二千多年，至今依然氣勢磅礴，雄偉壯觀。美國阿波羅宇航員阿姆期特朗首次登上月球時說過："從太空回望地球，用肉眼只能最清晰的辨認中國的萬里長城。"萬里長城的工程量確實驚人！據粗略的估計，若將明朝修建的長城所用的磚石、土方築成一道寬一米，高五米的大牆，能繞地球一周有余。如果用來鋪建寬五米，厚三十五厘米的公路，可以繞地球三、四周。這些數字充分體現了長城的工程量之雄偉巨大，在世界古建史上也是絕無僅有的，因而被評為世界七大奇迹之一。中國的萬里長城象座歷史的豐碑象征着中華民族的勤勞勇敢和頑強不息的精神。

　　而今，長城已成為世界旅游勝地，各國人民無不向往登上萬里長城一睹其雄姿，"不到長城非好漢"已成為中外游人的至理名言。北京的八達嶺、慕田峪，河北的山海關、金山嶺，天津的黃崖關，遼寧的九門口，山西的娘子關、雁門關，甘肅的嘉峪關等雄關隘口作為旅游熱點成為中外游客了解歷史熱愛中國的重要所在。萬里長城給錦繡中華增添了多少詩情畫意，春季，山花爛熳，萬紫千紅；夏季，層巒叠翠，霧里藏龍；秋季，漫山紅遍，層林盡染；冬季，冰封萬里，山舞銀蛇，把祖國山河點綴得燦爛奪目，使中外旅游者為之傾倒。長城不僅是中國的驕傲，也是全人類文化的瑰寶，更是聯系世界各國人民的友好紐帶。我們這本畫冊從旅游角度出發，把長城的風貌展現在讀者面前，願給讀者以美的享受；我們祝願每個登上長城的人，都成為眞正的好漢！

1996.1. 編者

Preface

The world-famous Great Wall lies in China as an enormous flying dragon. It starts from Yalu River bank in the east, through high mountains, vast stppes and boundless deserts, to reach at the snow-covered Tianshan Mountains in the west. The extraordinary difficult engineering and imposing manner of the Great Wall give a more magnificent scenery to Northern China. Great architecture of ancient China, the Great Wall is considered one of the wonders of the world, it holds a very important place in the history of the world civilisation. In 1988, the UN designated it one of the world's greatest cultural heritages. A crystallization of blood, sweat and intelligence, the Great Wall is not only a historical monument of China, but also a symbol of Chinese people.

The Great Wall, with a history of more than 2000 years, still keeps its imposing manner and looks magnificent today. When they arrived on the moon, American astronauts of the space-shuttle Apollo II said exitedly that the only man-made structure to be visible from the moon was the Great Wall of China. The engineering of the Great Wall is astonishing! According to a rough estimation, if you took all the bricks and rocks used in the Great Wall of the Ming Dynasty and built a wall 1 meter wide and 5 meters high, it wouid go around the earth once or more. If a highway 5 meters wide and 35 centimeters thick was built with those materials, it could go around the earth 3 or 4 times. The Great Wall is really a miracle of the worid!

The Great Wall is a great military defence project of ancien China. When Qin Shi Huang unified China in 221 B. C., he linked up the northern walls of the Qin, Zhao and Yan Kindoms to protect from the invasions of nomadic tribes of the North, while demolishing others. Stretching from Lintao (now Mingxian in Gansu Province) in the west to Liaodong in the east, the Great Wall had at that time a lenghth of more than 5,000 kilometers. As a solid defense system, it became more and more famous. The Great Wall was extended and rebuilt in the Han Dynasty. Streching from Yalu River bank in the east to Luobupo Lake in what is now Xinjiang autonomous region, it has a total lenghth of more than 10,000 kilometers, the longest in its history. Having gone through many changes, the Great Wall was reconstructed in a large scale in the Ming Dynasty. Extending westward from the Yalu River bank to Jiayuguan in Gansu Province, the Great Wall as we know today is mostly the construction of the Ming Dynasty with a total lenghth of about 6,350 kilometers. The Great Wall was built at top of the mountains, depicting beautiful curves of their ridges. Meandering along high mountains and deep valleys with its hundreds of passes and thousands of forts, watch towers in a hamony, the Great Wall is really magnificent, one can not help admiring the deligence, intelligence and greatness of the Chinese People.

The Great Wall had never ceased to be perfected from its beginning to its end of the role as a means of defence. Rising and declining along with the long history of China, the Great Wall lost gradually its original function, the erosion of wind and rain with the man-made dammage dilapidated the Great Wall. After the foundation of the People's Republic of China, the Great Wall was assigned one of the most important historical sites to be repaired. After restoration of many of its important sections, the Great Wall has resumed its imposing manner, it is now an important tourist attraction for people all over the world. The Great Wall is not only a pried of China, but also a tresor of the world civilisation and a link between peoples all over the world!

Janury 1996

前　書

　中国の大地において、世を挙げて、その名の聞こえる万里の長城が空を闊歩する巨竜のように、鴨緑江のほとりから西に向けて飛立ち、聳え立つ山山やはてもしない大草原を越え、広大な大漠を跨り、真っ白な雪に覆われる天山の麓に飛んで行った。その困難極まる厖大な工事と天を衡く勢いは北国の景色をいっそう絢爛たるものにしたのである。長城は中国古代の偉大な建築であり、世界建築史上の奇跡の一つとして世界文明の歴史に載せられ、一九八八年国連によって世界文化遺産と指定された。万里の長城は中国各民族人民の血と汗と智慧の結晶であり、中国の歴史における朽ない紀念碑とも言え、中華民族のシンボルとなっている。

　長城は中国の歴史において、二千年以上も活躍し、今日になってもあいかわらず勢いよく、雄大壮観そのものである。アメリカの宇宙船アポロが月に登った時、宇航士は「月で人間の目ではっきり見えたのは中国の万里の万城だけだった」と感激した。万里の長城の工事量はほんとうに驚くべきものであった。大雑把な統計によると、明の時代に長城を修築するのに使った石、煉瓦、土で、広さ1メートル、高さ5メートルの垣をつくるなら、地球を一周して余りがあるほどつくれるそうである。また広さ5メートル、厚さ35ミリの道をつくるなら、地球を三周も四周もできるほどである。中国の万里の長城はまことに世界の奇跡たるに恥じないものである。

　長城は中国古代の偉大な軍事防御工事でもあった。紀元前221年、秦の始皇帝は中国を統一してからそれまでに存在していた各国間の長城をすべて取り除けて、元の秦、趙、燕などの三国の北側にあった長城を結ばせ、北方の遊牧民族を防御した。この長城は西は臨洮（今の甘粛省岷県にあたる）から始まり、東は遼東まで全長1万華里余りもあって、堅固でうちやぶることのできない北方防御体系となり、万里の長城もその時から世に名が聞こえるようになった。漢の時代になって、秦の時代よりさらに発展させ、東は鴨緑江のほとりから、西はずっといまの新疆羅布泊まで延ばされ、全長は2万華里も越え、長城の史上最長期をなした。その後も長城は変遷をくりかえ、明の時代にふたたび大規模な長城修築が行われた。東は鴨緑江の入江から、西は甘粛省の嘉峪関まで、全長1万2700華里余りもあり、今日われわれが見える長城のほとんどはこの時につくられたものである。長城は大抵山の頂上につくられ、山の脊に沿って、曲りくねって尽きることのない山山の美しい曲線を浮彫りにした。長城の上にある無数の堅固で雄大な櫓と山頂に聳え立つ烽火台が遙かに向いあって呼応しあった。万里の長城はその雄大な勢いで、険しい山山の間を疾走し、数百の関所、要害や何千何万という堅固な櫓や烽火台と一体となって、中華民族の勤勉、智慧と偉大さで人人を感服させた。

　長城はつくられた時からくりかえされる改築と修繕を経て、歴史的な役割な完遂させるまで、ずっと中国の長い歴史と一緒にあゆみ、盛衰をともにしてきた。近代になって、長城はすでに本來の防御の役割をなくし、自然の風化と人為的な破壊で崩壊寸前となっていた。新中国が成立し、長城は重点的な修繕プロジエクトとして見なされた。すでに大事な部分が多く修復され、長城はふたたび昔の雄姿を見せるようになった。いま中国の長城はすでに世界的な観光地となった。長城は中国の誇りだけでなく、全人類の文化的珍宝でもあり、また世界各国人民をむすびつく友好的なきずなでもあった！

장 성

　중국대지애 구축된 세상에 널리 알려진 만리장성은 압록강반에서 날아올라 아아 뭇산과 망망한 초원을 넘고 드넓은 대사막을 지나 하얀 눈으로 뒤덮힌 천산기슭쪽으로 날아가는 한마리의 큰 룡을 방불케 한다. 만리장성은 그 류달리 어려운 공사와 람찬 기세로 중국 북녘땅의 풍경을 한결 더 아름답고 다채롭게 장식해주고 있다.

　중국 북부지역 유목민족의 침범을 막기 위해 구축한 장성은 중국 고대의 위대한 방어공사로서 기원전 7세기 춘추전국시대로부터 기원 17세기 명나라말기에 이르는 연 이천년이란 장구한 기간을 거쳐 완성된것이다. 전후로 20여개 왕조에 걸쳐 장성을 수축하였는데 그중에서 규모가 가장 큰것은 진시황이 중국을 통일하고 구축한 진나라 장성, 한나라 무제때 수축한 한나라장성, 명나라 태조때 쌓은 명나라 장성이다. 나라시기에 이르러 장성은 위소성과 진성, 로성, 영성, 변관, 돈대, 전대, 봉화대, 문 등 이름난 험요한 요새들을 갖춘 완전한 군사방어체계를 형성하게 되였는바 압록강어구에서 감숙성 가욕관에 이르는 그 총길이는 약 1만 2,700여리나 된다. 장성의 대부분은 산곡대기에 수축되였는바 산등성이를 따라 나가며 끝없이 구불구불 뻗어나간 산세로 하여금 아름다운 곡선륜곽을 이루게 하고 무수한 돈대들이 먼 산봉에 뚝 솟은 봉화대와 서로 호응되게 하였다. 험산준령숙에 만어있는 반리장성은 100애의 험요한 요충지, 수천수만개의 웅장한 돈대와 봉화대가 전일체롤 이룬 우람찬 기를 펼쳐보임으로써 사람들로 하여금 경탐을 자아내게 하고 근면하고 슬기롭고 걸한 중화민족의 위대성에 감복케 한다.

　만리장성은 구축된지 이미 2천여년이 되였지만 여전히 기세가 우람차고 웅위로운 장관이다. 미국의 아폴로 우주선 비행사 아무스트랑은 처음으로 달에 착륙하였을 때 《높은 하늘에서 지구를 굽어보니 육안으로 가장 똑똑히 가려 볼수 있는것은 중국의 만리장성뿐이다.》라고 말한바 있다. 만리장성의 공사량은 실로 사람을 놀려울 정도웇다. 대충 따져보아도 만일 명나라때 장성수축에 사용된 벽돌과 돌, 흙으로 너비 1메터, 높이 5메터의 큰 담벽을 쌓는다며 지구를 한바퀴 에돌고도 남는다고 한다. 그리고 만일 그것으로 너비 5메터, 두께 35센치메터의 도로를 건설한다면 지구를 서너바퀴나 에돌수 있다고 한다. 이 수자는 장성공사의 웅위함과 거대함을 충분히 구현함으로서 세계고대건축사에서도 극히 드문것이다. 하기에 만리장성은 세계 7대기적의 하나로 평가되였다. 중국의 만리장성은 력사적 불후의 걸작으로서 근면하고 용감하고 완강하고 꾸준한 중화민족의 정신웇 상징하고 있다.

　오늘 만리장성은 세계적인 유람승지로 되여 각국 인민들 모두가 만리장성에 올라 그 웅위로운 모습을 감상하려한다. 하여 《장성에 오르지 못하면 사내 대장부가 아니다》라는 말은 이미 국내외 관광객들의 명언으로 되였다. 베이징의 팔달령과 모전욕 하북의 산해관과 금산령, 천진인 황애관, 료녕의 구문구, 산서의 랑자관과 안문관, 숙의 가욕관 등 험요한 요충지들은 국내외 관광객들로 하여금 중국력사를 료해하고 중국을 사랑하게 하는 중요한 인기관광지로 되였다. 만리장성은 실로 아름다운 증에 수많은 시적인 광경을 부여해주었다. 만리장성은 봄철이면 산에 뭇꽃이 울긋불긋 피여나고 여름철이면 뭇산에 푸른 숲이 울창하고 안개속애 룡이 깃들인듯 하며 가을철이면 온산에 단풍이 지여 첩첩한 숲이붉게 물들고 겨울철이면 만리에 얼음 덮이고 은빛룡이 춤추는듯한 경관웇 이루며 조국의 산천을 눈부시게 장식하므로 국내외 광객들의 경탄을 아내개 한다. 만리장성은 중국의 자랑일뿐아니라 전인류 문화의 귀한 보배이기도 하며 또한 세계 각국 인민들간의 련계를 강화하는 친선의 뉴대이 도하다. 이화첩은 관광의 각도로부터 출발하여 장성의 모습을 독자들에게 펼쳐보이니 독자들이 미적향수를 만끽하기 바란다. 우리는 장성에 오르는 관광객들 모두가 진정한 사내대장부로 되여주기를 삼가 축원한다.

LA GRANDE MURAILLE

La Grande Muraille, célèbre dans le monde entier, se dresse comme un énorme agon en Chine. Elle part près du Fleuve Yalu, traversant vers l'ouest des hautes ontagnes, des vastes steppes et des deserts sans bornes, pour aboutir au pied es Montagnes Tianshan couvertes de la neige. Les travaux extrèmement pénibles de Grande Muraille et sa belle prestance embellient le Nord de la Chine. Gigantesque onstruciton de la Chine antique, la Grande Muraille est considérée comme un miracle ans l'histoire de construction du monde, elle occupe une placetrès importante dans la vilisation du monde. En 1988, l'Organisation des Nations unies l'a désignée comme des grands héritages culturels du monde. Resultat de la sagesse, du sang et de sueur du peuple Chinois, la Grande Muraille est non seulement un monument his-rique Chinois, mais aussi un symbole du peuple Chinois.

Bien que la Grande Muraille ait plus de deux milles ans d'histoire, elle garde en-ore sa belle prestance. Après avoir atterri sur la Lune, les astronautes américans de navette astronomique Apollo II dirent que la seule chose ils avaient pu distinguer ar l'oeil sur la Lune était la Grande Muraille de la Chine. Les travaux de construction e la Grande Muraille sont vraiment ètonnants! D'après l'estimation simple, si l'on con-ruise un mur d'une largeur d'un mètre et une hauteur de cinq mètres avec desgrosse iques et des blocs de pierres utilisés par La Grabde Muraille de La Dynastie des ing, il pourrait faire un tour de la Terre. Si l'on construise avec ces matériaux une utoroute d'une largeur de cinq mètres et une épaisseur de trente—cinq centimètres, le pourrait faire deux ou trois tours de la Terre. La Grande Muraille est vraiment e miracle du monde!

La Grande Muraille est une grande ouvrage de défense militaire de la Chine an-que. Après avour unifié la Chine en 221 av. j. —c. , l'empreur Shihuandi de la Dynas-e des Qin, relia les diverses murailles des anciens Royaumes de Qin, Zhao et Yan long de leur frontière nord des murailles pour se protéger des incursions des tribus omades, tout en détruisant les autres murailles des anciens royaumes. S'étandant, e l'ouest à l'est, de Lintao (aujourd'hui Minxian dans le Gansu) à Liaodong, la rande Muraille eut une longueur de plus de 5,000 kilomètres à cette époque. Ram-art imprenable au Nord de la Chine, elle devenait de plus en plus connue du monde. onsolidée et prolongée sous la Dynastie des Han, la Grande Muraille fut mesuree lus de dix milles kilomètres, partant auprès du Fleuve Yalu à l'est pour aboutir squ'au Lac Luobupo de Xinjiang a l'ouest, c'était la plus longue muraille ever con-ue dans son histoire. La Grande Muraille fut reconstruite d'une grande envergure sous Dynastie des Ming après avoir connu becoup de changements. S'étandant, de l'est l'ouest, de la gorge du Fleuve Yalu à la Passe Jiayuguan, la Grande Muraille que ous voyons aujourd'hui est à peu près la Grande Muraille de la Dynsatie des Ming vec une longueur de 6,350 kilomètres. La plupart de la Grande Muraille est constru-e sur les crêtes de montagnes, decrivant ainsi leurs belles lignes courbes. Serpent-ant dans les hautes montagnes et les vallers profondes, la Grande Muraille est plus tonnante avec ses centaines de passes et ses milliers de fortins et avant—postes. n ne peut s'empêcher devant elle d'admirer la diligence, la sagesse et la grandeur u peuple Chinois.

La Grande Muraille n'a pas cessé de se perfectionner depuis sa construction squ'à la fin de son role comme un moyen de défence. Connaissant des périodes de randeur et decadence le long de la longue histoire de Chine, la Grande Murailllle a erdu graduellement sa foncton originale elle a été dans une condition pitoyable à ause de l'erosion de vent et de pluie et la destruction causée by des gens. Après la ondation de la Republique Populaire de Chine, la Grande Muraille a été désignée omme un des plus importants sites historiques de la Chine à être protégés. Main-enant beaucoup de ses tronçons importants ont été reconstruits, la Grande Muraille est remise à sa prestance d'auparavant. Elle devient aujourd'hui un des importants ites touristiques du monde. Comme un lien entre les peuples du monde, elle est non eulement l'orgueil de la Chine, mais aussi le trésor du monde entier!

DIE GROSSE MAUER

Chinesen bezeichnen die Große Mauer gem als Drachen, und wie der Drachen ist sie ein Sym-ber chinesischen Nation. Dieses gewaltige Bauwerk, das Astronauten vom Mond aus mit bloßen Augen sehen konnten, erstreckt sich über 6350kilometer von der Mündung des Flusses Yalu in der provinz Liaoning im Osten bis zum paß Jiayuguan in der provinz Gansu im Westen. Der Mauerab-schnitt von Shanhaiguan in der provinz Hebei bis zur Mündung bes Flusses Yalu wurde, da nurein-fach ausgeführt, im Laufe der Zeit schwer in Mitleidenschaftgezogen, während der Abschnitt von Shanhaiguan bis Jiayuguan sehr fest gebaut und gut erhalten ist. An beiden Enden schließ die Große Mauer jeweils mit paß-Befestigungenab. Von der Bohai-Bucht östlich vom paß Shanhaiguan verläuft die Große Mauer in westlichen Richtung durch die Provinz Hebei, den Großraum Beijing, die provinz Shanxi, das Autonome Gebiet Innere Mongolei, das Autonome Gebiet Ningxia, die provinz Shaanxi und schließlich durch die provinz Gansu bis zum paß Jiayuguan.

Die Arbeiten für den Bau und wiederholte Restaurierungen sowie den Ausbau der Großen Mauer zogen sich über 2000Jahre hin. Im7. Jahrhundert v. Chr. begann man im Staat Chu eine quabratische Stadtmauer anzulegen. Während der Zeit der Frühlings-und Herbstperiode(770-476 v. Chr.)und der Streitenden Reiche(475-221 v. Chr.)bauten die Fürstentümer. Chu, Qin, Yan, Qi, Han, zhao, Wei und viele andere zur Verteidigung ihrer eigenen Territorien jeweils Schutzmauern. im 4. Jahrhundert V. Chr. bauten die Staaten Yan, Zhao und Qin an ihren nördlichen Grenzen hohe Mauern, um die Nomadenstämme aus dem Norden fernzuhalten. Der Qin-Kaiser Shi Huang Di, der 221 V. Chr. China einigte, ließdann diese einzelnen Mauern miteinander verbinden und ausbauen. Zu jener Zeit begann die Große Mauer im Westen bei Lintao in der Provinz Gansu und endete im östlichen Teil der provinz Liaoing. Sie erstreckte sich über eine Entfernung von 10 000 Li(1 Li= 500 Meter). So nennt man die Große Mauer auch die ″ Meuer von 10 000 Li″. in der darauffol-genden DYnastie wurde die Große Mauer dann noch weiter ausgebaut. in der Han-DYnastie wurde sie entlang der alten Seidenstraße nach Wseten verlängert. von Jiuauan über Dunhuang in der prov-inz Gansu bis nach Lop Nur im heutigen Uigurischen Autonomen Gebiet Xinjiang, wobei im Westen Xinjiangs auch Alarmfeuertürme, Festungen und andere Verteidigungsanlagen entstanden. Die Mina-Dvnastie war die letzte der Dvnastien, die an der Restaurierung und am Ausbau der Großen Mauer arbeiteten, und die Ming-Zeit war auch die Hochzeit für den Bau technisch perfekter Verteidi-gungsanlagen der Großen Mauer. Die Große Mauer der Ming-Dynastie erstreckte sich über 5660 Kilometer, und aus der Ming-Zeit(1368—1644)stammt auch das meiste, was von der Großen Mauer erhalten ist.

Beim Bau und Ausbau der Großen Mauer bewiesen die Chinesen Klugheit und Weisheit. Sie nutzten geschickt alle topographischen Gegebenheiten des Geländes aus, legte man an den strate-gisch wichtigen Stellen Befestigungen an und erfanden viele neue Methoden der Verwaltung, des Einsatzes der Arbeitskräfte, des Transports und der Versorgung mit Baumaterialien sowie der eigentlichen Bauausführung. Historischen Aufzeichnungen Zufolge beschäftigten sich über 20 Fürsten-tümer und feudale Dynastien mit dem Bau und Ausbau ber Großen Mauer. Die Mauern ber Qin-und der Han-und der Ming-Dynastie waren jeweils über 5000 Kilometer lang. Die in den verschiedenen Geschichtsperioden erbauten Großen Mauerm ergaben insgesamt eine Länge von ca 50 000 Kilo-metern. Mit den Steinen und den Mengen von Erdreich, die für den Bau der Großen Mauer allein in der Ming-Dynastie benutzt wurden, könnte man eien ein Meter dicken und fünf Meter hohen Wall rund um den Aquator errichten. Wenn man damit eine fünf meter breite und 35 Zentimeter dicke Straße anlegte, könnte sie viermal den Aquator umrunden. Die Großen Mauern aus allen Perioden, also 50 000 Kilometer, zusammengerechnet, so könnte der Wall zehnmal um den Aquator laufen und die Straße 40mal den Aquator umrunden. Ein so gigantisches Bauwerk wie die Große Mauer ist in der Weltgeschichte der alten Architektur beispiellos.

Die große Mauer diente im alten China als Verteidigungsanlage. Die über Berg und Tal dahinziehenden Mauerwände verbinden einige hundert Gebirgspäße und zehntausend Alarmfeuertürme sowie Wacht-und Kampftürme. Die Alarmfeuertürme wurden entlang bzw. innerhalb und außerhalb der Großen Mauer in bestimmten Abständen gebaut. Sie stehen meist auf höher gelegenen Stellen, aber in flachem Gelände mit weitem Blickfeld. Kam es zu einem feindlichen Angriff, so signal-isierten die Alarmfeuertürme bei Tag durch Rauch und nachts durch Feuer ihre Meldungen. Auf diese Weise konnte eine Meldung von Turm zu Turm bis zur großen. Verteidigungszone und zur Hauptstadt weitergeleitet werden. So entstand ein vollständiges Sigalsystem. Die quer über die Mauer gebauten Kampftürme sind zwei- oder dreistöckig. Die Wachmannschaften verfügten dort über Wohnräume und Depots für Waffen und Munition, um jederzeit kampffähig zu sein. Diese Türme wurden unter der Leitung Qi Jiguangs (1528—1587), eines berühmten Ming-Generals, zur Abwehr japanischer Seeräuber gebaut und spielten bei der militärischen Verteidigung eine bedeu-tende Rolle.

Die Große Mauer spielte in der Geschichte eine bedeutende Rolle für die politische, wirtschaftliche und kulturelle Entwicklung in Nordchina und für die Absicherung des Verkehrs, Han-dels und Kulturaustauschs mit westlichen Ländern. Inzwischen hat die Große Mauer zwar ihre ur-sprünglichen Funktionen verloren, doch als historisches Kulturdenkmal und für den Tourismus ist sie von allergrößtem Wert. Ein chinesisches Sprichwort heißt;, Wer nicht die Große Mauer bestiegen hat, der ist kein rechter Kerl. , Und wann besteigen Sie die Große Mauer.

金山嶺晨曲
Morning glow over the Great Wall.
朝焼け
Le jour point sur la Grande Muraille.
금산령의 아침
Die Große Mauer im Morgenschein.

長城日出
A Watch tower on the Great Wall at sunset.
夕日に照る城樓
Une toer au crépuscule.
장성의 해돋이
Ein Stadtmauerturm im Abendsonnenlicht

金龍狂舞
The Great Wall at Badaling looks like a giant dragon.
東方の巨竜
Le Grand Dragon de l'Orient.
흥겹게 춤추는 금빛룡
Wie ein riesiger Drachen erscheint hier die Große Mauer im Osten

夕照古長城
An ancient castle at dusk.
夕日に映える
Le soleil couchant.
석방빛 어린 옛장성
Alte Festung im Schein der untergehenden Sonne

古北口之夏
The Great Wall at Gubeikou in Summer
古北口の夏
Gubeikou en été
고북구의 여름
Sommerlandschaft des Mauerabschnitts
Gubeikou

龍延萬里
The Great Wall crosses many high mountains.
えんえんと続く長城
Un infatigable voyageur.
만리에 서린룡
Die Große Mauer windet sich über Berg und Tal

風起雲涌
The Great Wall at Jinshanling amidst clouds.
長城の雲海
La tempéte sur la Grande Muraille.
바람이일고 극름이 모여든다
Dem Sturm ausgesetzt(Mauerabschnitt in Jinshanling)

秋到長城
The Great Wall in autumn.
長城の秋景色
La Grande Muraille en automne.
가을철의 장성
Die Große Mauer im Herbst

長城初雪
An eatly snowfall.
初雪
Première neige.
장성의 첫눈
Nach dem ersten Schneefall

遠古之聲
An ancient city on a high mountain.
高山古城壁
La garde.
먼 옛날의 소리
Eine alte Festung

長城落日
Ancient city, new look.
古長城の新しい姿
Le nouvel aspect d'une ville ancienne.
장성의 락일
Altes Bauwerk mit neuem Antlitz

恆古久遠
The Great Wall at Jinshanling at sunset.
夕日に照る金山嶺
Le mont Jinshanling au crépuscule.
영구하리
Die Mauer auf dem Berg Jinshanling in der Abenddämmerung

古城暢想
Peepholes on the Great Wall.
城塞
La terreur de l'ennemi.
옛성을 즐겁게 감상
Schießscharten und Gucklöcher der Großen Mauer

長城初雪
An eatly snowfall.
初雪
Première neige.
장성의 첫눈
Nach dem ersten Schneefall

遠古之聲
An ancient city on a high mountain.
高山古城壁
La garde.
먼 옛날의 소리
Eine alte Festung

蒼龍戲水
Clouds over the Great Wall.
緑にかかる霧雲
Le charme de la Nature.
청룡의 물놀이
Ein in Wolken gehüllter Mauerabschnitt

八達嶺之晨
A bird's-eye view of the Great wall at Badaling.
八達嶺を見おろす
une vue de Badaling.
팔달령의 아침
Der Mauerabschnitt Badaling aus der Vogelperspektive

春山如笑
The Great Wall in May.
春の長城
Le printemps arrive sur la Grande Muraille.
봄날의 아름다운 경치
Frühlingsstimmung

望京樓夕輝
The Great Wall at Wangjinglou at sunset.
夕日に照る望京樓
Le mont Wangjinglou au crépuscule
석방빛 어린 망경루
Die Mauer auf dem Berg Wangjinglou in der Abenddämmerung

晴空萬里
The Great Wall sometimes disappears in clouds.
竜が伏しているかのような長城
Un dragon se cach dans le nuage.
끝없이 맑고 푸른 하늘
Die Große Mauer verschwindet ab und zu in Wolken

白雲越嶺
White clouds fly over mountains.
白雲がひろがる長城
Dans les nuages.
령을 넘는 흰구름
Weiße Wolken über der Mauer

盤山越嶺
The Great Wall runs along mountain ridges trom east to west.
東西に走る長城
Une course interminable.
만리에 뻗은 장성
Die Große Mauer schlängelt sich von Osten nach Westen durch Nordchina

風蝕古城
A great defense work.
鋼鐵のような防壁
Une barrière infranchissable.
풍식된 옛성
Stark befestigte Verteidigungsanlage

霧漫金山嶺
The Great Wall at Jinshanling shrouded in mist.
雲につつまれる金山嶺
La Grande Muraille à Jinshanling.
안개 서린 옛성
Der in Wolken gehüllte Mauerabschnitt auf dem Berg Jinshanling

長城之夏
The Great Wall at Mutianyu in Summer.
慕田峪の夏
Mutianyu en été.
장성의 여름
Sommerlandschaft des Mauerabschnitts Mutianyu

司馬臺長城
The Great Wall at Simatai.
司馬台長城
La Grande Muraille à Simatai.
사마대 장성
Der Mauerabschnitt in Simatai

八達嶺夜色
Brighe Moon over Badaling.
八達嶺日暮の月色
La pleine lune à la Badaling.
팔달령 야경
Der helle Mond uber dem Badaling

睡佛山長城
The Great Wall at Qingshankou.
青山口長城
La Grande Muraille à Qingshankou.
수블산 장성
Ein Abschnitt der Großen Mauer in Qingshankou

仙女樓霞光
Fairy Maid Tower wrapped in mist.
霧につつまれる仙女樓
La tour de la Déesse dans le brouillard.
노을 비낀 선녀루
Der in Nebel gehüllte Turm Xiannülou (Feen-Turm)

天高雲淡
The Great Wall at Mutianyu after rain.
雨あがりの慕田峪
Mutianyu après la pluie.
하늘은 높고 구름은 맑다
Der Mauerabschnitt Mutianyu nach einem Regen

盤山越嶺
The Great Wall winds through deep mountains.
えんえんと延びる長城
A travers les montagnes.
산을 넘고 령을 지나
Die Große Mauer zieht sich über hohe Berge dahin

銀裝素裹
The Great Wall wrappes in snow.
白銀の装い
La Grande Muraille sous la neige.
새하얀 소복차림
Ein schneebedeckter Abschnitt der Großen Mauer

龍臥翠嶺
The Great Wall on luxuriant mountains.
緑の山嶺に伏せる竜
Un dragon couché dans la verdure des montagnes.
룡이 엎드린 듯한 푸른령
Ein Mauerabschnitt auf einem grün bewachsenen Berg

敵樓高聳
A Watch tower on the Great Wall.
そびえ立つ城塞
La vigilence d'une tour de guet.
우뚝 솟은 고루
Ein auf dem Gipfel stehender Kampft

八達嶺暮色
The Great wall at Badaling at sunset.
八達嶺の夕暮れ
Badaling à la nuit tombante.
팔달령의 황혼
Die Mauer in Badaling in der Abenddämmerung

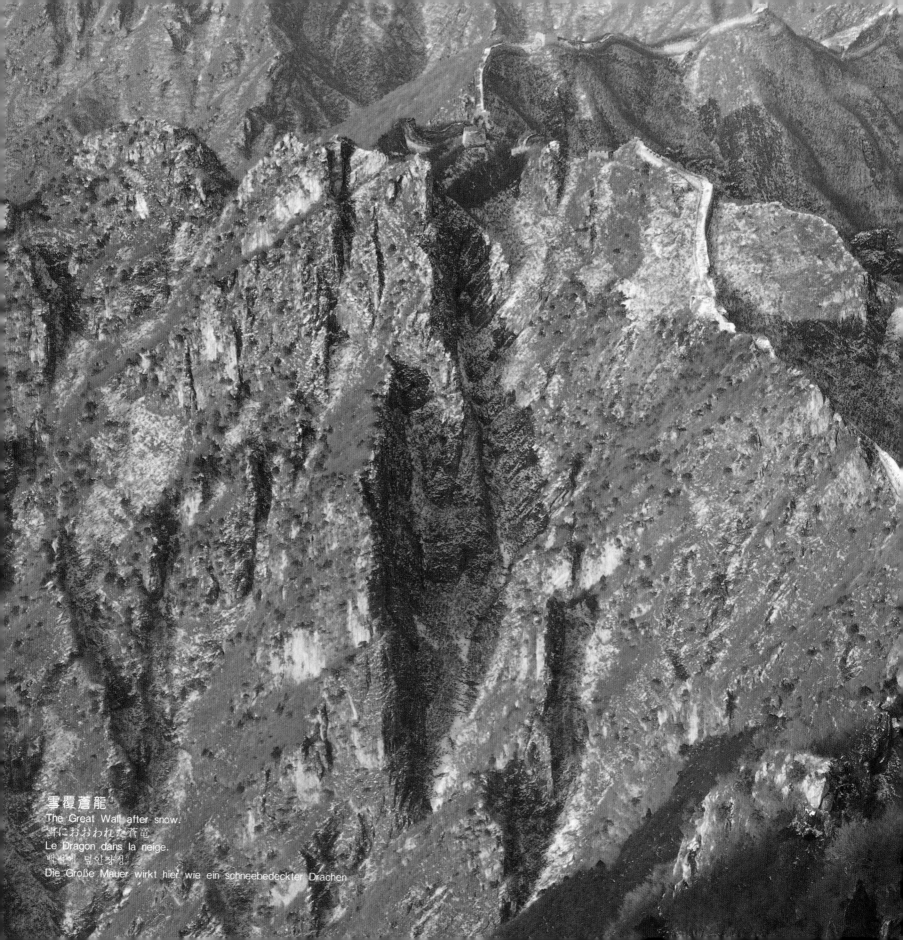

雪覆蒼龍
The Great Wall after snow.
雪におおわれた蒼竜
Le Dragon dans la neige.
백설에 덮인 장성
Die Große Mauer wirkt hier wie ein schneebedeckter Drachen

青山翠嶺
Reforestation has made the Great Wall much greener.
緑におおわれる長城
La verdure.
푸른 산과 령
Ein Mauerabschnitt auf einem bewaldeten Berg

巨龍騰飛
The Great Wall runs along mountain ridges.
舞う巨竜
L'essor d'un dragon géant.
날아 오르는 큰룡
Die Große Mauer klettert Berge hinauf wie ein
emporsteigender Drachen

山花爛熳
The Great Wall at Badaling in spring.
八達嶺長城の春景色
Le printemps sur la Grande Muraille de Badaling.
아름다운 꽃들
Der Mauerabschnitt Badaling im Frühling

雲起黃崖關
Tourists on the Great Wall at Huangyaguan.
黃崖關に遊ぶ
La joie de se promener à Huangyaguan.
황애관의 구름바다
Touristen auf der Großen Mauer am Huangya-Paß

古磚春意
Through the ages.
昔から今末で
De l'antiguité jusgu'à nos jours.
옛벽돌의 춘정
Die Mauer in Xifengkou，Provinz Hebei

歴盡滄桑
The Great Wall has seen numerous battles.
一部はすでに崩壊
La Grande Muraille a tout vu à travers les siècles.
상전벽해를 다겪다
Ein verfallener Mauerabschnitt-Zeuge vom Auf und Ab mehrerer Dynastien

司馬臺天梯
A Distant View of Fairy Maiden's Peak and
Heavenly Ladder in Sima Terrace.
遠いところから司馬臺仙女峰の天梯を眺める
Ici，la Grande Muraille devient un "escalier
menant au ciel".
사마대의 높은 사다리
Ein Blick vom Gipfel "Nimphen" bei Sima-
Terrasse her auf die "Himmel-Leiter".

勇攀八達嶺
The Great Wall at Badaling.
八達嶺長城
La Grande Muraille à Badaling.
팔달령에 오르다
Der Mauerabschnitt in Badaling

古堡殘冬
Watch towers on the Great Wall.
城塞林立
Une forêt de tours de guet.
옛성보의 늦겨울
Benachbarte Kampftürme

古城之夢
The mountains are covered with red leafs in autumn.
紅に染めるもみじ
Paysages d'automne.
옛성의 꿈
Herbstlandschaft mit der Großen Mauer

山舞銀蛇
The Great Wall in winter.
銀色の蛇が舞うかの上にそう長城
La danse d'un serpent d'argent.
Winterlandschaft an der Großen Mauer

城入雲顚
A strategic pass on the Great Wall in Jixian.
薊北の要害
La Grande Muraille dans le nord du district de Jixian，entre Eeijing et Tianjin.
구름 우에 솟은 성벽
Ein Abschnitt der Mauer an strategisch wichtigen Stellen in Jixian

古城瑞雪
The Great Wall.
のろし台が見える
La Grande Muraille à Jiankou.
옛성의 상서려운 눈
Der Mauerabschnitt Jiankou

殘雪藝趣
A storage tower on the Great Wall.
雪が降ったあとの鋪房樓
La neige sur une tour.
잔설의 예취
Ein schneebedeckter Kampfturm

長城之歌
The Great Wall at Badaling in autumn.
秋のもみじ
La montagne automnale.
장성의 노래
Der Mauerabschnitt Badaling im Herbst

水關臥龍
The Great Wall at Panjiakou.
潘家口長城
La Grande Muraille à Panjiakou.
와룡의 물놀이
Der Mauerabschnitt in Panjiakou

春城桃花
Blooming pear trees on the Great Wall.
滿開の梨の花
Les péchers fleurissent.
봄도시의 복숭아꽃
Ein Mauerabschnitt in schöner Umgebung mit blühenden Birnbäumen

望京樓晨霧
The Great Wall at Wangjinglou.
望京樓長城
La Grande Muraille à Wangjinglou.
만경 루의 아침안개
Der Mauerabschnitt in Wangjinglou

霧繞臥龍山
The Great Wall at Welongshan.
臥龍山長城
La Grande Muraille à Welongshan.
안개서린 와룡산
Der Mauerabschnitt in Welongshan

春報金山嶺
The Great Wall at Jinshanling.
金山嶺長城の威容
La splendeur de la Grande Muraille à Jinshanling.
봄을 맞은 금산령
Ein majestätischer Mauerabschnitt auf dem Berg Jinshanling

屹立千秋
The Great Wall has survived about 2,000 years.
そびえ立つ長城
A l'épreuve des siècles.
태연라이수
Seit über 2000 Jahren besteht die Große Mauer

燈火闌珊
The Dusk Great Wall at Mutianyu.
慕田峪長城の日暮れ時の景色
La Grande Muraille à Mutianyu à l'heure du crépuscule.
가물거리는 등불
Die Große Mauer unter der Abenddämmerung

翠嶺藏龍
The Great Wall at Mutianyu after rain.
雨あがりの慕田峪
Mutianyu après la pluie.
푸룽령에 깃든인룡
Der Mauerabschnitt Mutianyu nach einem Regen

殘牆挺立
The Great Wall of the Ming Dynasty in Dingbian.
明代の定辺長城
La Grande Muraille des Ming à Dingbian.
우뚝 솟은 낡은 땅벽
Ein Mauerabschnitt aus der Ming-Dynastie in Dingbian

流連忘返
Tourists on the Great Wall.
長城に遊ぶ
Des Visiteurs tout absorbés.
산수경치를 한껏 즐기라
Ein Höhepunkt jeder Chinareise ist ein Bereich der Großen Mauer

長城好漢

"One cannot be called a hero if he cannot reach the Great Wall".
萬里の長城に行かねば好漢にあらず
《One n'est pas héros sans monter sur la Grande Muraille.》
장성의 사내대장부
"Wer nicht die Große Mauer bestiegen hat，der ist kein rechter Kerl."

作者简介：

　　翟東風同志，是北京攝影圈內的后起之秀。由於他勤奮刻苦，杰作倍出，在攝影界中有很大的聲譽。現在是中國攝影家協會會員；中國藝術攝影協會會員；中國長城學會會員；北京長城攝影協會理事長。

　　1979 年，翟東風同志調公安部第一研究所，開始從事攝影專業，工作積極，任勞任怨。在完成本職工作的前提下，他很偏愛風光攝影，尤其對長城攝影興趣更濃，于是，他經常利用節假日時間，去長城進行攝影創作。幾年來，他爬遍了八達嶺、金山嶺、慕田峪、司馬臺，白天爬懸崖過絕壁，風餐露宿，晚上睡敵樓臥戰道，不分嚴寒酷暑，為國家拍攝了大量的珍貴資料。至今，他一直保持着這股充沛的創作熱情，廢寢忘食，夜以繼日，創作了許多優秀作品。特別近五年來，他除了報刊、雜志、以及各種畫冊上發表的若干作品外，還在不同題材的攝影藝術展覽中，連連獲獎。據不完全統計，僅榮獲三等獎以上的作品就有六十余件，始終名列前茅。

　　本書冊選用的照片，是作者在長城攝影中的部分作品，為了宣傳需要，有些作品不一定是作者的代表作，但是，它對宣傳長城起了很大作用，特向作者致意。

〔京〕新登字 176 号

责任编辑：杨显国
主　编：舒　辉
摄　影：翟东风
装帧设计：石国强
翻　译：余波（英、法）
　　　　赵家俊（日）
　　　　王素行（朝）
　　　　赵　谦（德）

图书在版编目（CIP）数据

长城/舒辉主编；翟东风摄影．—北京：中国民族摄影艺术出版社，1996.4
ISBN 7-80069-111-x

Ⅰ．长…　Ⅱ．①舒… ②翟…　Ⅲ．摄影集-中国-现代
Ⅳ．J426

中国版本图书馆 CIP 数据核字（96）第 04892 号

长城　　　　　　　　　舒辉编
中国民族摄影艺术出版社
开本：787×1092 毫米　　12 开　　印张：6
1996 年 3 月第 1 版　　1996 年 3 月第 1 次印刷
ISBN 7-80069-111-×/J.82
002600